365

Affirmations

To Smile

By Kelly Clanton

Symphony PUBLISHING

365 Affirmations to Smile

365 Affirmations to Smile

1. Self Help 2. Internet

E-book Version: Kindle
ISBN-13: 978-0692615621 (Symphony Publishing)
ISBN-10: 0692615628

To everyone who has inspired me and encouraged me to go after my dreams, I dedicate this book to you. From a small town in central Oklahoma, I fell in love with the thoughts and the words going through my mind. As I began to journal, the writings not only touched me, but they began to inspire friends and family. In those moments, I changed. I realized there is more to life than going through the motions of day-to-day living.

These affirmations were written to encourage and inspire you to smile every day, no matter your circumstances. This book is meant to be used as inspirational daily readings. However, I wanted to give you more than just my thoughts in this book. Therefore, I have made space for you to journal your inspiration or thoughts and have a reason to smile each day.

In a world with so much negativity, my passion is to inspire positive thoughts, one thought at a time. My hope is that I can inspire you! You can follow me and connect with me on Facebook at Reasons to Smile – Kelly Clanton.

Special thanks to my publisher, Jody Harris, Symphony Publishing, without you none of this would have come together.

3

January 1

☐ ☐ ☐ ☐ ☐

Your soul will search a lifetime for it; your mind will convince your heart you already have it. There the two shall war until the soul finds their other half and at that moment eternal peace is within.

_____

_____

_____

_____

_____

January 2

☐ ☐ ☐ ☐ ☐

He said: "I feel many words in a brief moment of deep thought while with you in conversation." She whispered: "Your thoughts are not unknown whether said or not, for they are my own."

_____

_____

_____

_____

_____

_____

January 3

□ □ □ □ □

Time to quit procrastinating!

_____

_____

_____

_____

_____

January 4

□ □ □ □ □

Never hate those jealous of you, for they think
you are amazing... always be yourself. The more
feelings you hide, the more they grow... find your
voice. In an instant, you can change your attitude
and change your entire day... direction
There is a blessing in everything!

_____

_____

_____

_____

_____

_____

January 5

☐ ☐ ☐ ☐ ☐

You don't always need a plan. Sometimes you just need to breath, trust and see what happens. Remind yourself it's ok to not be perfect. It's not selfish to love yourself. Take care of you and make your happiness a priority.

_____

_____

_____

_____

_____

January 6

☐ ☐ ☐ ☐ ☐

You know my name, not my story. You've heard what I've done, not what I've been through. Learn from yesterday, live for today and hope for tomorrow. Make memories you'll look back on and smile. Laugh as much as you breathe and love as long as you live.

_____

_____

_____

_____

_____

January 7

□ □ □ □ □

Every time you were completely convinced you couldn't go on... guess what, you did! Freedom is being yourself without anyone's permission. Don't let negative people hold you back. Do what makes you happy and be with who makes you smile.

_____

_____

_____

_____

_____

January 8

□ □ □ □ □

You opened up the corners of my mind and dusted all the cobwebs off. You've touched my heart and grabbed a hold of my soul.

_____

_____

_____

_____

_____

January 9

□ □ □ □ □

Life is available in the present
Live Simply
Dream Big
Be Grateful
Give Love
Laugh Often

_____

_____

_____

_____

_____

January 10

□ □ □ □ □

You fall, you rise, you make mistakes, you love, you
live and you learn. You are human, not perfect.
You've been hurt but you are here. What an
amazing privilege it is to be alive, to breathe, to
think, to enjoy and be around things you love.

_____

_____

_____

_____

January 11

□ □ □ □ □

Be around those that make you smile more than frown.

January 12

□ □ □ □ □

Sometimes there is sadness in our journey, but also great wonder.
Find it... See it... Feel it.
Always take the next step. You never know what is waiting just around the corner.

January 13

☐ ☐ ☐ ☐ ☐

Strive for progress, not perfection.
Every day is a second chance.

_____

_____

_____

_____

_____

January 14

☐ ☐ ☐ ☐ ☐

Our value doesn't decrease based on others
inability to see it.

_____

_____

_____

_____

_____

_____

January 15

□ □ □ □ □

It just takes one glance, a slight nod, a feeling like none other, and just like that we start all over again the next day... and life will happen in the in-between spaces.

_____

_____

_____

_____

_____

January 16

□ □ □ □ □

Life has no remote, you want something different get up and change it.

_____

_____

_____

_____

_____

_____

January 17

□ □ □ □ □

You are my passion, my reason, my escape.
Through you in me I can conquer the world and all
my dreams.

_____

_____

_____

_____

_____

January 18

□ □ □ □ □

We fear others not seeing our worth.
We want attention.
We crave presence.
Dream of peace within it all.

_____

_____

_____

_____

_____

_____

January 19

□ □ □ □ □

Learn to appreciate everything and regret nothing. Some of the best things happen when we least expect them. Use actions to back your words every chance you get. It is how they become truth.

_____

_____

_____

_____

_____

January 20

□ □ □ □ □

The struggles you are in today help build the strength you need tomorrow. Every accomplishment begins with trying.

_____

_____

_____

_____

_____

January 21

☐ ☐ ☐ ☐ ☐

Perfect isn't in any relationship, but if you have genuine love, respect, communication and understanding then it is perfect enough.

_____

_____

_____

_____

_____

January 22

☐ ☐ ☐ ☐ ☐

Love the people who make you laugh. At the end of the day, smile and be happy. It is contagious!

_____

_____

_____

_____

_____

_____

January 23

□ □ □ □ □

Always believe in yourself. Feelings change, people change, but memories are forever. Peace is within you. Love life, Live with no regrets, Smile, Laugh and Be Happy. No storm lasts forever and you're never alone in it.

_____

_____

_____

_____

_____

January 24

□ □ □ □ □

The goal isn't to live forever, but to create something that will.

_____

_____

_____

_____

_____

January 25

☐ ☐ ☐ ☐ ☐

Don't start your day with broken pieces of yesterday... Faith.

Never let a hard lesson harden your heart... Trust.

You can complain because roses have thorns or smile because thorns have roses... Perspective.

Someone is praying for the things you take for granted... Hope.

Trust your journey and surround yourself with ones that love you, smile often, belly laugh daily and just breathe.

_____

_____

_____

_____

_____

_____

_____

_____

_____

_____

January 26

□ □ □ □ □

The mind needs to hear the words.
The heart needs to feel the actions.
The soul already knows it all.

_____

_____

_____

_____

_____

January 27

□ □ □ □ □

Respect is earned,
Honesty appreciated,
Trust gained,
Loyalty returned,
Be thankful always!

_____

_____

_____

_____

_____

_____

January 28

□ □ □ □ □

What worries you, masters you… Hope.
Stop living in fear of making a mistake; learn and
grow from them… Strength.
Love always needs showing, not just words or
feeling… Actions.
True love will not betray you, but, instead, set you
free… Trust.
Follow your heart, but take your brain with
you… Courage.
Time is our most precious gift, so use it wisely and
with the right people… Faith.

_____

_____

_____

_____

_____

_____

_____

_____

_____

January 29

□ □ □ □ □

One simple positive thought to start your day can change everything.

_____

_____

_____

_____

_____

January 30

□ □ □ □ □

We make a living by what we get but make a life by what we give. Be kind, it costs nothing and the rewards are life altering.

_____

_____

_____

_____

_____

_____

_____

January 31

□ □ □ □ □

How much easier would it be to first blame others
for our situation? However, it is much more
productive to dig deep and search within ourselves.
The answers have always been there. Stop being
the victim and rise the victor.

_____

_____

_____

_____

_____

February 1

□ □ □ □ □

Make today amazing YOU are worth it!

_____

_____

_____

_____

_____

_____

February 2

□ □ □ □ □

Sometimes people will come into our lives for a shorter period than you would have liked, but teach us things they never could have had they stayed. Always take time out every day for those that matter most.

_____

_____

_____

_____

_____

February 3

□ □ □ □ □

Allow yourself to be silently tugged by what you love most... it will not forsake!

_____

_____

_____

_____

_____

February 4

□ □ □ □ □

There are blessings every day –
Find them, Create them and Treasure them.
Smiling for someone is great, but being the reason
they smile... Priceless.

_____

_____

_____

_____

_____

February 5

□ □ □ □ □

It doesn't matter how rich, talented or cool you
think you are. Your integrity and how you treat
others says it all. You have to water flowers daily
for them to last.

_____

_____

_____

_____

_____

February 6

□ □ □ □ □

Always be sure to love who you are. There will be plenty to hate... Believe.
Don't judge someone's choices before you know their reason... Compassion.
Don't put off what you can do today, you might not get tomorrow... Actions.

_____

_____

_____

_____

_____

February 7

□ □ □ □ □

Remember you are confined only by the walls you build. Find your hammer.

_____

_____

_____

_____

_____

February 8

□ □ □ □ □

Just because you may not get credit, you must never stop doing your best. Enjoy the little things, sometimes they end up being the big things. Live every day to the fullest and always be you... it is perfectly enough.

_____

_____

_____

_____

_____

February 9

□ □ □ □ □

Wake up every morning and put a smile on. You never know what a difference it could make!

_____

_____

_____

_____

_____

February 10

□ □ □ □ □

One's truth is no less truthful due to the number of people who believe it – stand strong!

_____

_____

_____

_____

_____

February 11

□ □ □ □ □

Embrace every day for what it is.
Be Happy,
Love Fiercely,
Smile Often.

_____

_____

_____

_____

_____

February 12

□ □ □ □ □

You should never underestimate the songs that find her... sometimes music just speaks volumes.

_____

_____

_____

_____

_____

February 13

□ □ □ □ □

Strength doesn't come through winning. Winning is just an end result. Going through hard times and not giving up is where your strength lies.

_____

_____

_____

_____

_____

February 14

□ □ □ □ □

Don't depend on people to build you up. You will give them the same power to tear you down... Reach within yourself!

_____

_____

_____

_____

_____

February 15

□ □ □ □ □

Be thankful for where you are, and keep fighting for where you want to be.

_____

_____

_____

_____

_____

February 16

☐ ☐ ☐ ☐ ☐

Your actions and words should always agree. If you
can't show it, don't say it.
Never push a loyal heart to the point they no
longer care.
The ones that know your heart will never have to
question it.

_____

_____

_____

_____

_____

February 17

☐ ☐ ☐ ☐ ☐

Do you want to be happy? Let go of what is gone.
Be grateful to what stays and look forward to what
is coming.

_____

_____

_____

_____

_____

February 18

□ □ □ □ □

In life, even the smallest steps can end up being the biggest. Walk lightly if needed, but take the step.

_____

_____

_____

_____

_____

February 19

□ □ □ □ □

Trust the timing in your life!

_____

_____

_____

_____

_____

_____

February 20

□ □ □ □ □

Two things define you:
Your patience when you have nothing and your
attitude when you have everything.
Everyone you meet has the ability to teach us...
what are you teaching?

_____

_____

_____

_____

_____

February 21

□ □ □ □ □

Smiling for someone is nice, but being the reason
they smile... Priceless!

_____

_____

_____

_____

_____

February 22

□ □ □ □ □

Don't look to others to change your life. Look in the mirror and know your worth. You are who you are today because of the choices you made yesterday.

_____

_____

_____

_____

_____

_____

February 23

□ □ □ □ □

Want Me, Need Me, Love Me.

_____

_____

_____

_____

_____

_____

February 24

□ □ □ □ □

At some point you have to let go of what you thought should happen and live in what is happening.

_____

_____

_____

_____

_____

February 25

□ □ □ □ □

Be what you love and don't bash what you hate. Once you accept your flaws, they can't be used against you. Define the definition of your life, not others. You only are in charge of your life and happiness; if you don't take the risk you'll never know what you're capable of.
Love like no tomorrow, but if it comes... love again.

_____

_____

_____

_____

_____

February 26

□ □ □ □ □

Every day we have a choice, be true to you and let others fall where they may.

_____

_____

_____

_____

_____

February 27

□ □ □ □ □

Thoughts become words, words your behavior, behavior turns into habit, habit turns into values and values are your destiny. Choose wisely!

_____

_____

_____

_____

_____

_____

February 28

□ □ □ □ □

Fierceness comes from desire that stems from a
need as a result of love... and the flow reverses.

_____

_____

_____

_____

_____

February 29 (Leap Day)

□ □ □ □ □

Love of Your Life vs. Soul Mate
One is a choice the other is not.

_____

_____

_____

_____

_____

_____

March 1

□ □ □ □ □

Someday someone will look at you with a fire in
their eyes that will stare straight into your soul – a
light so bright it will cause your heart to glow.
They'll look at you like you're everything they've
been looking for their entire life... Wait for it!

_____

_____

_____

_____

_____

March 2

□ □ □ □ □

Fill your Mind with Truth, your Heart with Love,
and your Life with Service.

_____

_____

_____

_____

_____

March 3

□ □ □ □ □

You don't get what you wish for, you get what you work for... what is it worth? If it's important, you find a way. If not, you find an excuse. Life is too short to wake up with regrets. Love the ones that treat you right and forgive the others to find your peace. Laugh your heart out, Smile always and cherish all the moments before they are memories.

_____

_____

_____

_____

March 4

□ □ □ □ □

In order to be irreplaceable one must be different. Don't be afraid to dance to your own beat. You never know the true value of a moment until it becomes a memory... Cherish the moments. In order to fly, you must first give up what weighs you down... Spread your wings.
When life is too hard to stand... Kneel.

_____

_____

_____

_____

March 5

□ □ □ □ □

Everything in your life is a result of a choice you made. Want different results? Make difference choices. You can't calm the storm, but you can calm yourself. The storm will pass. Faith is being sure of what we hope for and certain of what we can't see. Today is another day to get it right. Let go of what you can't change and embrace what you can.

_____

_____

_____

_____

_____

March 6

□ □ □ □ □

Until you give up the idea that happiness is somewhere else, it will never be where you are.

_____

_____

_____

_____

_____

March 7

□ □ □ □ □

Be yourself and aspire to be a giver.
Give Love,
Give Good Vibes,
Give Strength,
Give Positivity.

_____

_____

_____

_____

_____

March 8

□ □ □ □ □

I'm not 100% sure of the key to success, but I'm
100% sure the key to failure is trying to please
everyone.
Be who you were meant to be. You can't always wait
for the perfect opportunity. Take the one you have
and make it perfect.

_____

_____

_____

_____

_____

March 9

□ □ □ □ □

A year from now you'll wish you had started today.

_____

_____

_____

_____

_____

_____

March 10

□ □ □ □ □

In life, you have to do what makes you happy. Be
with ones that make you smile. Laugh as much as
you breathe. Love as long as you are living. Every
day is a new beginning – look to what it can do.

_____

_____

_____

_____

_____

_____

March 11

□ □ □ □ □

The truth isn't always beautiful, and beautiful
words aren't always truth.

_____

_____

_____

_____

_____

March 12

□ □ □ □ □

You can't influence the world by being like it... Get
out of your box. Happy people don't have the best
of every-hing; they make the best of what they
have. Be the type of people you want to meet.
Make someone look forward to tomorrow.

_____

_____

_____

_____

_____

March 13

□ □ □ □ □

When you judge someone you are defining yourself
not them.
Giving up isn't always weakness, sometimes it means
immeasurable strength.

_____

_____

_____

_____

_____

_____

March 14

□ □ □ □ □

The quieter you become, the more you can hear.

_____

_____

_____

_____

_____

March 15

□ □ □ □ □

Speak words of kindness. Be careful, the tongue is sharp. Seek out good in others so they may see it in you. Forgive, even if they aren't sorry. Forgiveness is for you, not them. Great relationships are built daily. Never stop working for it.
Life is better laughing!

_____

_____

_____

_____

_____

March 16

□ □ □ □ □

Life is full of give and take... Give thanks and take nothing for granted. You never need a reason to help someone.

_____

_____

_____

_____

_____

March 17

□ □ □ □ □

Believe in yourself, even if no one else does. They don't define you. Don't allow your problems to steal your happiness.
Dream it... Faith.
Believe it... Hope.
Create your sunshine... Love.

_____

_____

_____

_____

March 18

□ □ □ □ □

You may not be there yet, but you are closer then yesterday... Faith. Don't let past mistakes bog you down. Rise up, shake it off and learn from it. Today is a whole new day.
Be what you want in other people... you can't keep expecting them to be more.
A smile is the best thing to put on every morning.

_____

_____

_____

_____

March 19

□ □ □ □ □

We can' change everything we face, but nothing
can change un⁺il we look to it... Take your step.

_____

_____

_____

_____

_____

March 20

□ □ □ □ □

Overthinking will destroy your mind and confuse all
your thoughts. Walk away from negativity and
drama, sit back and watch beautiful things happen.
A simple smile can cure a multitude of ailments...
Use it.

_____

_____

_____

_____

_____

_____

March 21

□ □ □ □ □

There is always something to be thankful for... Find it!

_____

_____

_____

_____

_____

March 22

□ □ □ □ □

Don't let selfishness bring unbalance.
Be good, it comes back around.

_____

_____

_____

_____

_____

_____

March 23

□ □ □ □ □

Pray hardest when it's hardest to pray... Faith.
Count the rainbows, not the thunder... Positivity.
Let your smile change the world. Never the other
way around... Compassion.
Nobody has everything, but everyone has
something... Perspective. You'll find happiness when
you stop comparing yourself to others....Believe
When your mind is ready to give up, hope whispers
one more time... Listen.

_____

_____

_____

_____

_____

March 24

□ □ □ □ □

Be faithful in small things, for it is within them
your faith lies.

_____

_____

_____

_____

_____

March 25

□ □ □ □ □

There are no shortcuts to anything worth having.
Thank your past for the lessons, and go get your
dreams. Walk slowly, but never backwards.

_____

_____

_____

_____

_____

March 26

□ □ □ □ □

Grudges are a waste of perfect happiness that
hurts you not them... Choose happiness.
Let your past make you better not bitter focus on
today. Mistakes are just proof you're trying.
Turn your words into wisdom. Sometimes what we
fear most ends up setting us free... FLY.

_____

_____

_____

_____

_____

March 27

☐ ☐ ☐ ☐ ☐

Fear kills more dreams than failure ever will... Keep Dreaming.

_____

_____

_____

_____

_____

March 28

☐ ☐ ☐ ☐ ☐

Character is how you treat those who can do nothing for you... Kindness.
Be silently drawn by the strange pull of what you love. Finc positivity in every day – all you have to do is look. What worries you controls you... Let go!

_____

_____

_____

_____

_____

March 29

□ □ □ □ □

No matter your circumstances in life, look up.
Tough at times, yes, but it is life. Up is the only
way to go.

_____

_____

_____

_____

_____

March 30

□ □ □ □ □

Home no longer was a place, but a feeling all
wrapped up in his arms.

_____

_____

_____

_____

_____

March 31

□ □ □ □ □

Once you encounter the one you were supposed to meet, conversation will take flight as if on wings of angels. They will have locks for your keys and keys for your locks. They will leave an imprint on your soul that anyone entertained after you will have to know you in order to know them.

_____

_____

_____

_____

_____

April 1

□ □ □ □ □

Sometimes our lives have to be shaken up a bit – moved around to put us where we need to be. Look ahead and always smile. You never know what a change it can make.

_____

_____

_____

_____

_____

April 2

□ □ □ □ □

Live every moment, Laugh every day, Love beyond words.

_____

_____

_____

_____

_____

April 3

□ □ □ □ □

Never forget the highest appreciation is not to just speak the words, but to live by them. We can't start the next chapter if we are hung up on the last. Fate whispers, "You can't stand the storm." But you whispered, "I am the storm." Remember what you are made of.

_____

_____

_____

_____

_____

April 4

□ □ □ □ □

Faith makes it possible; hope makes it work; love makes it beautiful... Let it be your perspective. Those that want it find a way. Those that don't find the excuse... Don't live in your head. Strength comes from knowing your weakness, wisdom from being foolish and laughter from sadness... Growth. Smile often, Dream big, Laugh a lot and realize how blessed you are!

_____

_____

_____

_____

April 5

□ □ □ □ □

I'd rather have a life of "Oh wells" than "What ifs."
Isn't it great when the things we can't change end up changing us... Embrace It!

_____

_____

_____

_____

_____

April 6

□ □ □ □ □

Happiness is in your heart, not the circumstances. How many people would you impress if the whole world was blind?

_____

_____

_____

_____

_____

_____

April 7

□ □ □ □ □

Be yourself to free yourself.

_____

_____

_____

_____

_____

_____

April 8

□ □ □ □ □

Remember, no storm lasts forever... Brave the rain.
Sometimes you find yourself in the middle of
nowhere. Other times, in the middle of nowhere
you will find yourselves.....Faith.
Distance yourself from the negative and feel peace
all around you... Freedom.
We all fit into someone's puzzle... Trust it.

_____

_____

_____

_____

_____

April 9

□ □ □ □ □

You choose your happiness. Smile, laugh and spread
it around.

_____

_____

_____

_____

_____

April 10

□ □ □ □ □

I hide my tears when I say your name.
But, the pain always remains the same.
The smile on my face tries to stay.
But, the truth is, no one misses you more than me.

_____

_____

_____

_____

_____

April 11

□ □ □ □ □

The most attractive thing anyone can do is exactly
what they said they would.

_____

_____

_____

_____

_____

_____

April 12

□ □ □ □ □

One smile can change a friendship.
One laugh can conquer gloom.
One touch can show you care.
One heart can lift a soul.
One word can change everything.
Be That One.

_____

_____

_____

_____

_____

April 13

□ □ □ □ □

Be happy in every moment. Stop, Listen and find
the joy, it is always there!

_____

_____

_____

_____

_____

April 14

□ □ □ □ □

Smiling can be the best way to face any problem,
handle any fear and hide any pain.
Your life has many chapters; one bad chapter
doesn't mean the end of the book... Turn the page.

_____

_____

_____

_____

_____

_____

April 15

□ □ □ □ □

Happiness can be found in the darkest of times.
Surround yourself with people that bring out the
best in you. Life is too short!
For all you have lost... You have gained.

_____

_____

_____

_____

April 16

□ □ □ □ □

Music feeds the soul, calms the heart and speaks to the mind.

_____

_____

_____

_____

_____

April 17

□ □ □ □ □

Surround yourself with people who will be there when it rains – not just when it shines.

_____

_____

_____

_____

_____

_____

April 18

□ □ □ □ □

You are not what has happened – you are what you
have chosen to become... Be wise.
We both lose and find ourselves in the things we
love... Be passionate.
Promote what you love instead of bashing what you
hate... Compassion.

_____

_____

_____

_____

_____

April 19

□ □ □ □ □

The need to want and be wanted, to have and be
had, to feed my hunger and my soul simultaneously.

_____

_____

_____

_____

_____

April 20

□ □ □ □ □

Your patience is not your ability to wait. It is your attitude while doing so. We often forget happiness isn't about getting what we don't have, but appreciating what we do have. You are what you do, not what you say you will do. Actions express priority. Be better today than you were yesterday and you have succeeded.

_____

_____

_____

_____

_____

April 21

□ □ □ □ □

A goal without a plan is just a wish – if you want it, work for it.

_____

_____

_____

_____

_____

April 22

□ □ □ □ □

Life isn't about being perfect, but you can be
happy with what you have. It is a choice. Learn
from yesterday, live for today and hope for
tomorrow. Hope anchors our soul. Don't look to
where you fell, look to where you stumbled.
Forgiveness doesn't change the past, but it can
widen the future.

_____

_____

_____

_____

_____

April 23

□ □ □ □ □

Some things are not meant to be understood, but
rather heard... Be willing to listen.
The strongest people aren't the ones that give up...
Look forward and keep going.

_____

_____

_____

_____

April 24

□ □ □ □ □

We are all part of someone's puzzle, find out where
you fit. When your mind wants to give up, hope
whispers "not yet..." hear it. Your struggle is part
of your story... Wear it proudly.

_____

_____

_____

_____

_____

April 25

□ □ □ □ □

There is no love without forgiveness and no
forgiveness without love.
Blessings are all around – find them, create them
and treasure them.

_____

_____

_____

_____

_____

April 26

□ □ □ □ □

Prayer in action is love.
Love in action is service.
Turn your wounds into wisdom.
Shine the way you were meant to.

_____

_____

_____

_____

_____

April 27

□ □ □ □ □

Be sure and taste your words before you spit them
out. Once said, they can't be taken back.
Select your battles; sometimes peace is more
important than being right.

_____

_____

_____

_____

_____

April 28

□ □ □ □ □

We tend to judge others by behavior and ourselves
by intentions. You can forget what hurt you, just
don't forget what it taught you. Everyone we meet
knows something we don't.

_____

_____

_____

_____

_____

April 29

□ □ □ □ □

Choose positivity in your life and surround yourself
with those that will be there when it rains not just
when it shines. One day they will be what you value
most.

_____

_____

_____

_____

_____

April 30

□ □ □ □ □

There is no peace by avoiding situations.
Hope is the only thing greater than fear.
Life is tough – Be tougher.
The greatest failure is simply not to try.

_____

_____

_____

_____

_____

May 1

□ □ □ □ □

Love is giving someone the power to break you, yet
trusting them to fix you.
Listen to your heart, it knows... Hear its silent tug.

_____

_____

_____

_____

_____

_____

May 2

□ □ □ □ □

Faith believes when it is beyond the power of
reason to do so.
A Heart, a Smile, a Person can leave an imprint no
one else can fill.

_____

_____

_____

_____

_____

May 3

□ □ □ □ □

We are all a little broken and rough around the
edges. We want someone to show us tomorrow isn't
just another day.

_____

_____

_____

_____

_____

May 4

☐ ☐ ☐ ☐ ☐

The past is behind you... Let it go.
The future isn't here yet... Be ready for it.
The present is here and now... Grab hold and live it.
What you do matters, but the why is your reason.

_____

_____

_____

_____

_____

May 5

☐ ☐ ☐ ☐ ☐

Someone is always grateful for the things you take
for granted.
Doing what is right isn't always easy, but always
worth it in the end.
Learn to trust your journey, even when you do not
understand it.
Free Yourself.

_____

_____

_____

_____

May 6

□ □ □ □ □

Find quiet alone time each day. It does good to refresh.

_____

_____

_____

_____

_____

May 7

□ □ □ □ □

Fill your mind with the truth, your heart with unconditional love and your life with one of service. You know you're on the right track when you no longer feel a need to look back.
Right now, this very moment, life is perfect

_____

_____

_____

_____

_____

May 8

□ □ □ □ □

People change for two reasons: you learn enough
and you want to, or you've been hurt enough and
have to. When things don't add up, start
subtracting. Actions that don't back up words are
empty words.

_____

_____

_____

_____

_____

May 9

□ □ □ □ □

Make your smile change the world instead of the
world changing your smile –
no regrets, just lessons learned.

_____

_____

_____

_____

_____

May 10

□ □ □ □ □

Life is about learning from yesterday, living for today and hoping for tomorrow. Let your strengths overcome your insecurities. Always make them wonder how you're smiling. Have courage enough to pursue your dreams.

_____

_____

_____

_____

_____

May 11

□ □ □ □ □

You never realize how strong you are until being strong is the only option you have. Don't stress over what you can't change, distance yourself from the negativity and let the positive start happening.

_____

_____

_____

_____

_____

May 12

□ □ □ □ □

Gratitude; you have it in you to recognize all the
good in your life.

_____

_____

_____

_____

_____

May 13

□ □ □ □ □

Some people you meet make your laugh a little
louder, your smile a little brighter, and your life
just better. Those are your people... They're the
ones worth holding onto.

_____

_____

_____

_____

_____

May 14

□ □ □ □ □

If you want something, you will find a way. If not,
then it will be an excuse... WANT IT!
If you wait until you're ready, you will always be
waiting... GET UP, MOVE FORWARD!
Behind every setback is the opportunity... WHAT
IS YOURS!

_____

_____

_____

_____

_____

May 15

□ □ □ □ □

Everyone you meet has something to teach.
Learning is a gift, even when pain is the teacher.
Remember, strong people stand up for themselves,
but stronger people stand up for those that can't.

_____

_____

_____

_____

_____

May 16

□ □ □ □ □

Be good to others and smile, you simply never know
what a difference you could make.

_____

_____

_____

_____

_____

May 17

□ □ □ □ □

In the end, most things just don't matter. Be
aware with how much you loved, how respectfully
you lived and how unapologetically you let go of
things not meant for you.

_____

_____

_____

_____

_____

_____

May 18

□ □ □ □ □

Don't judge a path you haven't walked.
Running away from problems is a race you will never win. What happens today can improve your tomorrows. When you are happy, the music beats inside you. When you are sad, the lyrics speak to you.

_____

_____

_____

_____

_____

May 19

□ □ □ □ □

Worry looks around; Regret looks back; Faith looks forward. Tomorrow isn't here; yesterday is gone; but today is NOW.

_____

_____

_____

_____

_____

May 20

□ □ □ □ □

Day by day you think nothing has changed in life, but when you stop a moment to reflect, everything is different. Anything you truly want must be worth the fight.

_____

_____

_____

_____

_____

May 21

□ □ □ □ □

How you think determines how you feel. How you feel influences the way you act. Think wisely, believe nothing is impossible and never dull your sparkle.

_____

_____

_____

_____

_____

May 22

□ □ □ □ □

Difficult doesn't mean impossible. It just means
you have to work harder.

May 23

□ □ □ □ □

A good life is when you smile often, dream big,
laugh a lot and understand how blessed you are for
what you have.

May 24

□ □ □ □ □

Train your mind to see the good in everything.
Don't hate what you don't understand. Don't regret
your past, it made you who you are.
Love is what makes us smile even when we are
tired.

_____

_____

_____

_____

_____

May 25

□ □ □ □ □

Anyone can promise the stars, but only you can
reach them.
Believe in yourself.

_____

_____

_____

_____

_____

May 26

□ □ □ □ □

Happiness isn't what makes us grateful, but rather gratefulness that makes us happy. Every day there is something good to see. Most of the time, listening is all someone needs.

_____

_____

_____

_____

_____

May 27

□ □ □ □ □

Live your life and forget your age.
Laugh at yourself. You'll always be amused.
Beauty is simplicity.

_____

_____

_____

_____

_____

May 28

☐ ☐ ☐ ☐ ☐

What you allow will continue. Can you remember who you where before the world told you who to be? Be a voice not an echo. Trust in YOU!

_____

_____

_____

_____

_____

May 29

☐ ☐ ☐ ☐ ☐

I am strong because I have been weak.
I am wise because I have known great sorrow.
I laugh because I've had immeasurable pain.
Positivity is a choice made daily. Actions express your priorities. You can't solve your problems using the same thoughts that created them.

_____

_____

_____

_____

_____

May 30

□ □ □ □ □

The most powerful weapon is the human soul on
fire. Be who you were meant to be and you'll set
the world ablaze with it.

_____

_____

_____

_____

_____

May 31

□ □ □ □ □

There will come a time where you realize what
matters to you, what never did and what always
will. Life is simply better when you are laughing.

_____

_____

_____

_____

_____

June 1

□ □ □ □ □

Surround yourself with those that bring out the best in you, not the stress in you. Being positive is always a choice.

_____

_____

_____

_____

_____

June 2

□ □ □ □ □

Courage is not the absence of fear, but, rather, the thought that something else is more important.

_____

_____

_____

_____

_____

June 3

☐ ☐ ☐ ☐ ☐

Everything happens for a reason.
Maybe the journey isn't so much about
becoming anything.
Live it, Love it, Learn from it.
Life is better laughing.

_____

_____

_____

_____

_____

June 4

☐ ☐ ☐ ☐ ☐

Be someone's solid landing – the place they can
come with all their thoughts and always find
comfort. For that is one of life's greatest
compliments.

_____

_____

_____

_____

_____

June 5

□ □ □ □ □

Don't stress over people or things in your past,
there is a reason why they didn't make it to your
present. Be in this moment and take time to enjoy
the simple thing life has given you.

_____

_____

_____

_____

_____

June 6

□ □ □ □ □

Life is about balance.
Be kind, but not a doormat.
Trust, but do not be deceived.
Be confident, but never stop improving.
Live for what tomorrow has to bring, not for what
yesterday has taken.

_____

_____

_____

_____

June 7

□ □ □ □ □

The way you think is how you feel and the way you feel is how you act. Learn to love yourself for what you are instead of hating yourself for what you're not.

_____

_____

_____

_____

_____

June 8

□ □ □ □ □

Being defeated is often a temporary condition. Giving up is what makes it permanent. What you do today can make all your tomorrows better. If it is important, you'll find a way.

_____

_____

_____

_____

_____

June 9

□ □ □ □ □

Train your mind to see GOOD in Everything.

_____

_____

_____

_____

_____

June 10

□ □ □ □ □

Your past is done. Remember what it taught you.
Your future isn't here yet – dream about it.
Your present is NOW. Live it with no regrets and
be happy.

_____

_____

_____

_____

_____

June 11

□ □ □ □ □

If you're always racing from one moment to the next, what happens to the one you're in? You know you're on the right track when you have no interest in looking back.

_____

_____

_____

_____

_____

June 12

□ □ □ □ □

Discipline is just choosing between what you want now and what you want most. Life doesn't have to be perfect to be wonderful.

_____

_____

_____

_____

_____

June 13

□ □ □ □ □

Make the rest of your life the best of your life.
Turn your cant's into cans and your dreams into plans.
Be You, Regret Nothing.

_____

_____

_____

_____

_____

June 14

□ □ □ □ □

Our best teachers are our past mistakes, learn from them and grow.
We are products of our past but we don't have to be prisoners of it.

_____

_____

_____

_____

_____

June 15

□ □ □ □ □

Life is about moving forward, accepting things
simply for what they are and looking to what makes
you stronger and more complete.

_____

_____

_____

_____

_____

June 16

□ □ □ □ □

You aren't defeated when you lose. You are only
defeated when you quit.
Never let fear decide your future.

_____

_____

_____

_____

_____

June 17

□ □ □ □ □

Life is way better when you're laughing. It is your choice whether to scream or enjoy the ride.

_____

_____

_____

_____

_____

June 18

□ □ □ □ □

Doing what you love is freedom. Liking what you do is happiness.

_____

_____

_____

_____

_____

June 19

□ □ □ □ □

Intelligence without a focus towards anything is like a car without brakes.

_____

_____

_____

_____

_____

June 20

□ □ □ □ □

All things fall into place when they should. Until then, laugh at the silliness, live for the moments and know everything happens for a reason.

_____

_____

_____

_____

_____

June 21

□ □ □ □ □

You don't need people to validate you. You're already valuable. Don't wish for something to happen – GO make it happen!

_____

_____

_____

_____

_____

June 22

□ □ □ □ □

I love people who make me smile – yes, it really is just that simple.

_____

_____

_____

_____

_____

June 23

□ □ □ □ □

There comes a point in your life when you realize
who really matters. Follow your heart, but take
your brain with you.

_____

_____

_____

_____

_____

June 24

□ □ □ □ □

When someone jumps to accuse you of things you
feel haven't been done, which road do you take?
Do you apologize or stand your ground? What if
you apologize but they still won't let go and
continue to treat you the way they have claimed
you treated? Listen to your heart but realize you
can't be the only one willing for the sake of others
feelings.

_____

_____

_____

_____

June 25

▢ ▢ ▢ ▢ ▢

Don't look back when you know you shouldn't. Don't
stress over things that won't matter. Don't worry
about things you can't control.
Respect is earned. Honesty is appreciated. Trust is
gained. Loyalty is returned.

_____

_____

_____

_____

_____

June 26

▢ ▢ ▢ ▢ ▢

May your life preach more loudly then your lips.

_____

_____

_____

_____

_____

_____

June 27

□ □ □ □ □

Sometimes the greatest act of faith is simply getting up and facing another day. When you love what you have, you have it all. Accept it for what it is worth. Lose yourself in it, for you will find yourself.

_____

_____

_____

_____

_____

June 28

□ □ □ □ □

Being positive in a negative situation is not naïve, it is great success. The key to failure is trying to please everyone else.

_____

_____

_____

_____

_____

June 29

□ □ □ □ □

Near or far is merely perception. How you feel and act means the same in either place. Love is what makes you smile, even when you are tired.

_____

_____

_____

_____

_____

June 30

□ □ □ □ □

When you start to wonder if you can trust someone, it is then you already have your answer. Be smart enough to hold on and brave enough to know when it is time to let go.

_____

_____

_____

_____

_____

July 1

□ □ □ □ □

Pain is Real... So is Hope.

_____

_____

_____

_____

_____

July 2

□ □ □ □ □

Ignore the ignorance of others. Give your energy
to things that matter. Don't let someone's
pettiness steal your happiness.

_____

_____

_____

_____

_____

July 3

□ □ □ □ □

Love will not leave you, it will set you free. Love is
an action, not just a set of words or a feeling.

_____

_____

_____

_____

_____

July 4

□ □ □ □ □

To choose to make a difference in the world, you
must first be different from the world.

_____

_____

_____

_____

_____

July 5

☐ ☐ ☐ ☐ ☐

Your past cannot be changed, forgotten, rewritten
or deleted, so choose your words and actions
carefully. They will leave a lasting impression that
can be both good and bad. Always be true to
yourself. Only a few will remain true to you.

_____

_____

_____

_____

_____

July 6

☐ ☐ ☐ ☐ ☐

Thankfulness is the beginning of happiness.

_____

_____

_____

_____

_____

July 7

□ □ □ □ □

Don't let the selfish need of others become your reality. Take charge in how you feel... Choose freedom.
Beautiful things happen when you walk away from the negative.

_____

_____

_____

_____

_____

July 8

□ □ □ □ □

You may not be there yet, but you're closer than you were yesterday.

_____

_____

_____

_____

_____

July 9

□ □ □ □ □

Without communication, there is no relationship.
Without true respect, there is no love. Without
real trust, there is no reason to continue. Don't let
anyone break you down with words of their own
selfishness.

_____

_____

_____

_____

_____

July 10

□ □ □ □ □

Sometimes we are led into troubled waters not to
overwhelm us but to renew us.......silence your mind,
the soul knows what to do.

_____

_____

_____

_____

_____

July 11

□ □ □ □ □

You have survived 100% of everything in your life so far. So there is a pretty good chance you'll survive what is next. Souls heal, restlessness goes away and you're always stronger then what you think. Don't let the delusions of others dictate who you are.

_____

_____

_____

_____

_____

July 12

□ □ □ □ □

Every scar has a story – don't be afraid to tell it. It made you who you are.

_____

_____

_____

_____

_____

July 13

□ □ □ □ □

There are two kinds of people you will meet in life.
Some will pick you up, dust you off and lift you
higher; others will step on you to keep you down. In
the end you will thank them both.

July 14

□ □ □ □ □

Smile, don't sweat the small stuff. We all make it
somewhere in the end.

July 15

□ □ □ □ □

Every storm runs out of rain. Every night turns to day. Every heartache goes away.
Forget what hurt you, but never what it taught you.

_____

_____

_____

_____

_____

July 16

□ □ □ □ □

When things aren't adding up, start subtracting. Be with the ones that show you love daily without hesitation. They are your heart, soul and blessings.

_____

_____

_____

_____

_____

July 17

□ □ □ □ □

We tend to lose sight of the fact that happiness doesn't come because of what we want, but, instead, from accepting what we have.

_____

_____

_____

_____

_____

July 18

□ □ □ □ □

Pain doesn't show up in our life for no reason. It is a sign something needs to change... Take back control over you.

_____

_____

_____

_____

_____

July 19

□ □ □ □ □

Don't let yesterday take up too much of today. It is a perfect time to start moving forward.

_____

_____

_____

_____

_____

July 20

□ □ □ □ □

Believe in yourself and aspire to be a giver.
Give love.
Give peace.
Give compassion.
Life has no remote. Get up and change it yourself.

_____

_____

_____

_____

_____

July 21

□ □ □ □ □

Always end the day with a positive thought.

_____

_____

_____

_____

_____

July 22

□ □ □ □ □

Not everything that is faced can be changed, but nothing changes if we sit back doing nothing. Face what is yours to face, head held high.

_____

_____

_____

_____

_____

_____

July 23

□ □ □ □ □

Learn it is not what you have, but who you have in
your life that counts at the end of the day.

_____

_____

_____

_____

_____

July 24

□ □ □ □ □

As hard as it is to change ourselves, why do we get
so discouraged when others don't fit our mold? Be
yourself, no one else can.

_____

_____

_____

_____

_____

July 25

□ □ □ □ □

What is done is done. What is gone is gone. One of life's lessons is to always move forward. Love those that treat you right and forgive those who don't.

_____

_____

_____

_____

_____

July 26

□ □ □ □ □

Sometimes we end up broken and shaken before we shine. Never give up. Always trust your heart.

_____

_____

_____

_____

_____

July 27

□ □ □ □ □

Love is looking at them and seeing all you've ever wanted. Their laugh is utterly contagious. Their smile makes you giddy for no reasons at all. The late night talks that make the morning arrive way too soon. Their jokes have you bursting with laughter days later. How they simply make your day better, even when you wanted to shut the world out. It is for every second you get to spend with them, even if those seconds leave you longing for more. Loving them makes you realize you've never loved before and will never love again the same way.

_____

_____

_____

_____

_____

_____

_____

_____

July 28

□ □ □ □ □

Maybe it's not always about trying to fix brokenness. Maybe it's about starting over – making something better with what is important.

_____

_____

_____

_____

_____

July 29

□ □ □ □ □

Open minded people welcome being wrong. They're free of illusions. They don't worry what people think of them.
Know your worth. It is greatness.

_____

_____

_____

_____

_____

July 30

□ □ □ □ □

Be smart enough to know when to stay and brave
enough to know when to go. Once you choose to
forgive those who hurt you, you take away their
hold over you.

_____

_____

_____

_____

_____

July 31

□ □ □ □ □

Pay attention to people's actions and you'll never be
fooled by their words.

_____

_____

_____

_____

_____

_____

August 1

□ □ □ □ □

It is truly amazing what happens when you let go of negativity and drama. Your days just become easier and better.

_____

_____

_____

_____

_____

August 2

□ □ □ □ □

The greatest feeling is your soul on fire = pure passion.
Those whose heart beats with ours hold onto.

_____

_____

_____

_____

_____

August 3

□ □ □ □ □

Choose to be happy because it is good for your health.
I have arrived, I am home, I am solid, I am free.

_____

_____

_____

_____

_____

August 4

□ □ □ □ □

There comes a time when turning the page feels so good, because it is freeing to realize there is so much more than the page you were stuck on.

_____

_____

_____

_____

_____

August 5

□ □ □ □ □

Ability is what we are capable of.
Motivation determines what we do about it.
Attitude shows how much we want it.

_____

_____

_____

_____

_____

August 6

□ □ □ □ □

Don't sit back and let things happen to you, go out
and happen to things. If you get to the end of your
rope, tie a knot and hang on.
Get your fire back!

_____

_____

_____

_____

_____

August 7

□ □ □ □ □

Awake.
Blessed.
Grateful.

_____

_____

_____

_____

_____

August 8

□ □ □ □ □

You can't make the same mistakes over and over;
they are no longer mistakes but choices.
Forgiveness doesn't mean continued acceptance.
Treat them how you want to be treated.

_____

_____

_____

_____

_____

August 9

□ □ □ □ □

There are far better things ahead than any we
leave behind.
Move forward, learn, love and laugh.

_____

_____

_____

_____

_____

August 10

□ □ □ □ □

You are never too old to set another goal or dream
a new dream.
Each step may be hard, but keep going
the view is beautiful.

_____

_____

_____

_____

_____

August 11

□ □ □ □ □

If you can lie down at night knowing in your heart you made someone's day better, that's when you know you have had a good day.

_____

_____

_____

_____

_____

August 12

□ □ □ □ □

People won't notice your tears.
People won't notice your sadness.
People won't notice your pain.
But they will notice your mistakes.
So quit worrying about the people that won't notice and get to loving the people that do. Love yourself so you know what you deserve.

_____

_____

_____

_____

August 13

□ □ □ □ □

One of the best feelings is someone who
appreciates everything about you that the others
took for granted.

_____

_____

_____

_____

_____

August 14

□ □ □ □ □

Truth sounds like hate to those that hate truth.
Be kind to the unkind, they need it the most.

_____

_____

_____

_____

_____

August 15

□ □ □ □ □

What comes out of your mouth reveals the person
you are – listen and speak from your heart.

_____

_____

_____

_____

_____

August 16

□ □ □ □ □

You can't change how people feel about you – that
is there's to feel.
Live your life, be happy and stay close to anything
that makes you glad to be alive.

_____

_____

_____

_____

_____

August 17

□ □ □ □ □

Work together passionately. Always remember the reasons that brought you here to begin with.

_____

_____

_____

_____

_____

August 18

□ □ □ □ □

A million feelings, A thousand thoughts, A hundred memories.
ALL that make me wish I could stop time.

_____

_____

_____

_____

_____

August 19

□ □ □ □ □

You have it in you to help others understand they matter... USE IT!

_____

_____

_____

_____

_____

_____

August 20

□ □ □ □ □

We can't just talk about our problems and expect change. Be a doer, be the solution.

_____

_____

_____

_____

_____

August 21

□ □ □ □ □

Life is full of people making mistakes – make sure
you're one of the ones learning from them.
If you can't improve the deafening silence, don't
speak.

_____

_____

_____

_____

_____

August 22

□ □ □ □ □

Everything in life reflects choices we make. If you
want something different, you have to make
different choices.
Let go of what doesn't make you happy and
embrace what does.

_____

_____

_____

_____

_____

August 23

□ □ □ □ □

My mind needs your thoughts.
My body needs your touch.
And it all sets fire to my soul!

_____

_____

_____

_____

_____

August 24

□ □ □ □ □

Speak your heart. If they don't understand it, it
was never meant for them.

_____

_____

_____

_____

_____

_____

August 25

☐ ☐ ☐ ☐ ☐

The first time I saw you. my soul gasped. My heart
fluttered, whispering, "he's the one."

_____

_____

_____

_____

_____

_____

_____

August 26

☐ ☐ ☐ ☐ ☐

When you wonder where someone's loyalty lies –
you already know the answer.

_____

_____

_____

_____

_____

August 27

□ □ □ □ □

You can suffer the fear of change or remain
stagnant in who you are... Take the step.

_____

_____

_____

_____

_____

August 28

□ □ □ □ □

That is what I've held onto, that is what has kept
me going forward. You, your love and my intense
need for you in my life always. The years of love
I've tucked into my soul. It is all that has fed me
along this journey.

_____

_____

_____

_____

_____

August 29

☐ ☐ ☐ ☐ ☐

Respect yourself enough to let go of what no
longer feeds your soul.

_____

_____

_____

_____

_____

August 30

☐ ☐ ☐ ☐ ☐

Love the people who make you laugh; it can cure a
multitude of ills. At the end of the day, before you
close your eyes, smile. Be happy where you are,
remember where you've been and be grateful for
what you have.

_____

_____

_____

_____

_____

August 31

□ □ □ □ □

How people treat others says a lot about how they
view themselves.
Be good, it comes back around.

_____

_____

_____

_____

_____

September 1

□ □ □ □ □

You are brave because you fought hard and won.
You are strong because you had to be.
You are happier because you learned what matters.
You stand taller because you are a survivor.

_____

_____

_____

_____

_____

September 2

☐ ☐ ☐ ☐ ☐

Before you assume, talk to them.
Before you judge, ask why.
Before you hurt someone, step in their shoes.
Before you speak, think.

_____

_____

_____

_____

_____

September 3

☐ ☐ ☐ ☐ ☐

Happiness is feeling good enough about yourself
that you no longer feel the need for others
approval.
Faith – it does make things easier and possible.

_____

_____

_____

_____

_____

September 4

☐ ☐ ☐ ☐ ☐

Guard your heart from the harshness of others.
Cry if you need to but pick yourself up and keep
going. Only a few people care to really know the
chapters in your book of life.

_____

_____

_____

_____

_____

September 5

☐ ☐ ☐ ☐ ☐

The day is what you make it.
Choose to make it Great and Wondrous.
Choose to smile, to love, to sing and to dance.

_____

_____

_____

_____

_____

September 6

□ □ □ □ □

Count blessings, not problems. Your hardest times
often lead to the greatest moments of your life.
Keep the faith; it will all work out in the end.

September 7

□ □ □ □ □

The people you step on today may be the very ones
you need tomorrow. A positive attitude can change
so much.

September 8

□ □ □ □ □

Sweet words come easy.
Sweet things anyone can buy.
Life ends when you stop dreaming.
Hope when you stop believing.
Love when you stop caring.
Friendship when you stop sharing.
Let your heart forgive freely and don't hurt the
heart that loves you.

_____

_____

_____

_____

_____

September 9

□ □ □ □ □

Dare to do just what you do, be just what you are
and dance as often as you can.

_____

_____

_____

_____

_____

September 10

☐ ☐ ☐ ☐ ☐

You'll never know bravery if you don't understand
pain.
You'll never grow if you don't fall.
You'll never be successful if you don't experience
failure.
We should take our own breath every once in a
while.

_____

_____

_____

_____

_____

September 11

☐ ☐ ☐ ☐ ☐

You are in control of what kind of day you're going
to have. It is not your circumstance that keeps you
unhappy, it is how you choose to respond to them.

_____

_____

_____

_____

_____

September 12

□ □ □ □ □

If you always take the easy way out and give up, you'll never know how strong you really are. No matter how hard it seems, make the decision to keep pushing forward.

_____

_____

_____

_____

_____

September 13

□ □ □ □ □

You were given this life because you are strong enough to handle it. Happiness is an inside job. Never outsource it to anyone.
Rise up and attack the day with enthusiasm.

_____

_____

_____

_____

_____

September 14

☐ ☐ ☐ ☐ ☐

Being happy in what you have doesn't mean all is perfect, it just means you decided to look beyond any imperfections.

_____

_____

_____

_____

_____

September 15

☐ ☐ ☐ ☐ ☐

Your mind is a powerful thing. When you fill it with positive thoughts, your life will start to change.

_____

_____

_____

_____

_____

September 16

□ □ □ □ □

Be awakened by all that is within you. Don't be afraid or back down from what you want. Your heart and soul will never allow your mind to rest until you go forth with that fierceness inside you. Find yourself and know your worth.

_____

_____

_____

_____

_____

September 17

□ □ □ □ □

In case you were wondering, the best way to get things done is to begin. Make sure it challenges you so it can change you. You don't become great by your comfort zone. Get outside of your box and shine.

_____

_____

_____

_____

_____

September 18

□ □ □ □ □

Don't just sleep with your dreams. Dare to wake up and chase them.

_____

_____

_____

_____

_____

September 19

□ □ □ □ □

When you try to be everyone else's anchor, you don't realize you're actually drowning yourself. Jump ship and make your happiness a priority. It is only then that you can be of help to anyone else. Seek peace.

_____

_____

_____

_____

_____

September 20

□ □ □ □ □

When you try to control everything, you enjoy nothing.
Relax, Enjoy, Live, Love, Laugh!

_____

_____

_____

_____

_____

September 21

□ □ □ □ □

Bad days happen. Sadness affects us all. Sometimes, it isn't a good day. That's ok, just let it be a day. Go through the motions of "a day" and let tomorrow be better. Each day after is closer to a good day. Until then... Just have a day!

_____

_____

_____

_____

_____

September 22

□ □ □ □ □

To give love to others we must first give love to
ourselves. It is only then that we will truly feel.

_____

_____

_____

_____

_____

September 23

□ □ □ □ □

You have to choose who to be; no one will come
hand it to you. Want it. Fight for it. You are the
only one that knows what you want. No one is going
to come save you. Save yourself. Don't live a life of
sorry; go get your dreams!

_____

_____

_____

_____

_____

September 24

□ □ □ □ □

Live your life from your heart, it will never steer
you in the wrong direction.

_____

_____

_____

_____

_____

September 25

□ □ □ □ □

Grief never ends, it changes form. It is a passing
through without a place to sit. It can be emptiness
so great we don't know how we'll move. It is not a
sign of weakness, nor a lack of faith, but quite the
opposite. It is the price of love.

_____

_____

_____

_____

_____

September 26

□ □ □ □ □

Decide today will be the day you wake up and say,
"I don't want to feel like that ever again" ...and
don't.

_____

_____

_____

_____

_____

September 27

□ □ □ □ □

Don't make a promise just because you're happy for
a moment.
Don't respond when you are angry and don't make
decisions when you are sad.

_____

_____

_____

_____

_____

September 28

□ □ □ □ □

Keep telling yourself you don't have to do what
everyone else is doing. Believe in yourself. Soon
the day will come when others will have no choice
but to believe.

_____

_____

_____

_____

_____

September 29

□ □ □ □ □

Anything that made you feel something taught you
something.
Don't hold on longer then you should, no matter
how it ended.

_____

_____

_____

_____

_____

September 30

☐ ☐ ☐ ☐ ☐

It is time to break free from those that do so little for you yet control so much of your mind and feelings. Be fearless. Know your worth. Saying goodbye only makes you stronger and opens doors you otherwise wouldn't see... Leap of Faith.

_____

_____

_____

_____

_____

October 1

☐ ☐ ☐ ☐ ☐

We aren't perfect; mistakes are made. Sometimes, I'm not the best friend. But, I wake up every day trying harder than the yesterday.

_____

_____

_____

_____

_____

October 2

□ □ □ □ □

The way you treat yourself will set the standard
for how others will treat you.
Be Good To Yourself!

_____

_____

_____

_____

_____

October 3

□ □ □ □ □

Life begins when we step out of our comfort zone.
Learn to love who you've become and fight hard to
keep it. Happiness is always a choice – choose it!

_____

_____

_____

_____

_____

October 4

☐ ☐ ☐ ☐ ☐

Be in love with your life... Every minute of it.

_____

_____

_____

_____

_____

_____

_____

_____

October 5

☐ ☐ ☐ ☐ ☐

Don't get down because you're having some rough times. Let it remind you just how strong you are! Know everything will be fine. Look how far you have come – keep plowing ahead!

_____

_____

_____

_____

_____

October 6

□ □ □ □ □

Day by day, we start to realize it isn't so much about the "things." We have or our pride, but it's more about who our heart beats for.

_____

_____

_____

_____

_____

October 7

□ □ □ □ □

Realize your worth; know its ok to walk away from what doesn't make you better. Showing your value isn't a weakness, it is a strength – always know your worth.

_____

_____

_____

_____

_____

October 8

□ □ □ □ □

We all have the ability to make someone happy. Use your gifts for good. Never miss the opportunity to make someone smile.

_____

_____

_____

_____

_____

October 9

□ □ □ □ □

Just when you think all is lost and everything is falling apart, turn the corner and realize it was all falling perfectly in place.
Trust your journey!

_____

_____

_____

_____

_____

October 10

□ □ □ □ □

We aren't meant to be perfect, we are meant to keep trying. Each day we are given another chance, take it. Make it your own, and always find the good in it. Through this you will become perfect enough.

_____

_____

_____

_____

_____

October 11

□ □ □ □ □

The beginning in anything we do is always the hardest – don't give up. Each day we truly want it, it will become easier. Believe in the person you want to become.

_____

_____

_____

_____

_____

October 12

□ □ □ □ □

A bad yesterday doesn't mean it won't be a good
today.
Breathe in the day, relax and say "I've got this!"

_____

_____

_____

_____

_____

October 13

□ □ □ □ □

We always talk about the courage it takes to
forgive someone, but what about the courage it
takes to ask for forgiveness? Never underestimate
the power of both.

_____

_____

_____

_____

_____

October 14

□ □ □ □ □

Today is the day! What does it mean to you? How does it speak your name? Are you listening? Are you getting closer to where you want to be?
Today is your day!

_____

_____

_____

_____

_____

October 15

□ □ □ □ □

Be so busy on your grass you'll never notice if theirs is greener. When you open your eyes to look around, life is pretty amazing – Perceptive.

_____

_____

_____

_____

_____

October 16

□ □ □ □ □

We must all be fearless in what sets our soul on fire. Look deeply with eyes blazing and hearts burning, and in that moment your mind will understand all it wants and needs.

_____

_____

_____

_____

_____

October 17

□ □ □ □ □

Being unstoppable simply means to believe in you.
What's stopping you?
Once you believe you can – you will!

_____

_____

_____

_____

_____

_____

October 18

□ □ □ □ □

Stars don't shine without darkness, but we weren't meant to live there. Never dull your sparkle.

_____

_____

_____

_____

_____

October 19

□ □ □ □ □

Better days are coming. They are around every corner. When you love yourself, you teach others what you deserve. Go after all your dreams and keep smiling.

_____

_____

_____

_____

_____

October 20

□ □ □ □ □

Have hope things will get better and strength to
hold on until they do.
It is ok to lean on others; it is called friendship.

_____

_____

_____

_____

_____

October 21

□ □ □ □ □

Be a blessing.
Be someone's deepest desire.
With all the want and need within you blazing in
your eyes,
with just their thought in your mind.
Let your heart guide you to your destiny.

_____

_____

_____

_____

_____

October 22

□ □ □ □ □

We find it hard to be happy because we tend to see the past as better than it was and our present less than it is – causing our future to seem bleak at most.

_____

_____

_____

_____

_____

October 23

□ □ □ □ □

Learn to let the simple things in life put a smile on your face. It is then you will be truly happy.

_____

_____

_____

_____

_____

October 24

□ □ □ □ □

If making someone happy costs your happiness,
then it is a cost you cannot afford – know your
worth.

_____

_____

_____

_____

_____

_____

October 25

□ □ □ □ □

How amazing it is when we find who we are – even
better when it's being happy with what you find.
Don't stop discovering.

_____

_____

_____

_____

_____

October 26

□ □ □ □ □

It is ok to say NO, there is no guilt in it. Learn to say YES to you! Let it free you.

_____

_____

_____

_____

_____

_____

October 27

□ □ □ □ □

Don't be fooled into thinking you need someone else to be happy. That thinking will lead to everyone's unhappiness.

_____

_____

_____

_____

_____

October 28

☐ ☐ ☐ ☐ ☐

She laid down with wolves knowing she would rise
up the leader of the pack.
Be Fierce in Showing Fearlessness!

_____

_____

_____

_____

_____

October 29

☐ ☐ ☐ ☐ ☐

Our strength doesn't lie in how much we can handle
before breaking, but in what we must bear once
broken.

_____

_____

_____

_____

_____

October 30

□ □ □ □ □

If you choose to wake up thinking little of yourself, you can be sure the world won't rise any higher. You have it within you to set your value.

_____

_____

_____

_____

_____

October 31

□ □ □ □ □

Proudly wear your scars – they are the story of all you survived. Never forget who you are and what you are made of.

_____

_____

_____

_____

_____

November 1

□ □ □ □ □

When we can smile in the morning like we weren't
crying last night... Our strength is defined.

_____

_____

_____

_____

_____

_____

November 2

□ □ □ □ □

Everything you've been through up to this moment
has all been about what is yet to come. You can't
break diamonds.

_____

_____

_____

_____

_____

November 3

□ □ □ □ □

Life has a funny way of making us humble - of
showing us it is ok to laugh at ourselves. Don't let
the world make you hard, Pain make you hate or
sorrow steal your joy. Keep smiling and make them
wonder.

_____

_____

_____

_____

_____

November 4

□ □ □ □ □

Don't give your power away. A smile that has
struggled through tears is beautiful.

_____

_____

_____

_____

_____

November 5

☐ ☐ ☐ ☐ ☐

Be someone's first and last thought each day.
Smiling is wonderful, but being the reason someone
smiles is priceless.

November 6

☐ ☐ ☐ ☐ ☐

Let go of what or who broke you. Focus on who
made you smile again... Keep that!

November 7

□ □ □ □ □

Arrows are only shot forward; when you feel life tugging you back, don't worry, stay focused and hang on for the ride. Never stop aiming!

_____

_____

_____

_____

_____

November 8

□ □ □ □ □

How easy is it for us to talk about our problems and gossip? How great would it be if we talked more about our joy? Try it!

_____

_____

_____

_____

_____

November 9

□ □ □ □ □

The very thing we are most afraid of could be the thing that sets us free. Old ways won't open new doors. We can't find anything in the same place we lost it.

_____

_____

_____

_____

_____

November 10

□ □ □ □ □

The ones that stand by your side, not ignoring, not wavering but, doing instead of just talking, they deserve your time, trust, heart and love. Don't be so guarded that you fail to see what's right in front of you.

_____

_____

_____

_____

_____

November 11

□ □ □ □ □

What consumes your mind controls your life. Make it good!

_____

_____

_____

_____

_____

November 12

□ □ □ □ □

Sometimes we have to stop chasing the wrong things, accept what is and move on... Life.

_____

_____

_____

_____

_____

_____

November 13

□ □ □ □ □

Revenge is a senseless emotion. It will only work to bring you down. You can't force someone that doesn't want the same things as you do or can't see the hurt in their actions. If it comes, let it. If it stays, great. If it is leaves, say goodbye. Don't allow them you suffering.

_____

_____

_____

_____

_____

November 14

□ □ □ □ □

Just because you let go doesn't mean you don't love them anymore. It just means you love yourself more. You are worth it.

_____

_____

_____

_____

_____

November 15

□ □ □ □ □

What becomes your passion becomes your reason.
It's a beautiful thing. Don't stop working for what
you can't stop thinking of.

_____

_____

_____

_____

_____

November 16

□ □ □ □ □

Stop focusing on the problems and see the
possibilities. No one said it would be easy, but it
will always be worth it. Scream, if you must, but
never give up.

_____

_____

_____

_____

_____

November 17

□ □ □ □ □

Keep going! You are getting there. Each day is closer than the last. Let your faith be bigger than your fear. You have all you need within you.

_____

_____

_____

_____

_____

November 18

□ □ □ □ □

What you are isn't what holds you back, but what you perceive you're not. Be your own fan club – your own motivation... Think happy!

_____

_____

_____

_____

_____

November 19

□ □ □ □ □

Be the person who lifts up and encourages others.
You never know who is silently struggling. Someday,
you may need the same kindness in return.

_____

_____

_____

_____

_____

November 20

□ □ □ □ □

What makes you stand out from the rest of the
world? We all have a unique gift to offer. Is yours
collecting dust? Do people look at you and say,
"because of you I didn't give up?" Find your gift.
Use it, inspire, you have what it takes.

_____

_____

_____

_____

_____

November 21

☐ ☐ ☐ ☐ ☐

How can we be happy if we hold onto things that make us sad? Don't give up your peace trying to convince someone of the hurt they caused – some just don't see their behavior.

_____

_____

_____

_____

_____

November 22

☐ ☐ ☐ ☐ ☐

Don't lose yourself trying to find someone – seek peace.

_____

_____

_____

_____

_____

November 23

□ □ □ □ □

If you don't believe in the person you want to become, who will? Be fearless in your pursuit and others will follow.

_____

_____

_____

_____

_____

_____

November 24

□ □ □ □ □

We all should hug a little longer, forgive sooner and love harder. In the end, we'll be glad we did.
Be the reason someone smiles today.

_____

_____

_____

_____

_____

November 25

□ □ □ □ □

The only thing you can control about a situation and its outcome is your attitude. Don't let your light be dimmed, but remember to be humble.
Forgive what needs forgiven so you can move forward.

_____

_____

_____

_____

_____

November 26

□ □ □ □ □

The meaning of life is to give life meaning. You are your only limit in doing so.

_____

_____

_____

_____

_____

_____

November 27

□ □ □ □ □

Sometimes we need to get out of our own head so we can keep going. Don't be so worried about falling, what if you fly!

_____

_____

_____

_____

_____

_____

November 28

□ □ □ □ □

Every morning start with "I CAN DO THIS!" Remember your reasons and let them be your focus. Show the world your confidence; it starts with believing in YOU!

_____

_____

_____

_____

_____

November 29

□ □ □ □ □

Life is not just a story, but many chapters in a
book. Don't lay it down. You'll never know the
ending.

_____

_____

_____

_____

_____

November 30

□ □ □ □ □

Keep fighting through the bad days. Show anyone
who says you can't that YOU CAN!

_____

_____

_____

_____

_____

December 1

□ □ □ □ □

Sometimes you win, sometimes you learn. Don't be afraid of life's darkness. That is when your light shines.

_____

_____

_____

_____

_____

December 2

□ □ □ □ □

There are heroes all around us. Look in the mirror and become yours.

_____

_____

_____

_____

_____

December 3

☐ ☐ ☐ ☐ ☐

Don't worry about what could go wrong; smile about
what can go right.

_____

_____

_____

_____

_____

December 4

☐ ☐ ☐ ☐ ☐

Everyone is fighting an unseen battle. You can
break us down temporarily, but we will pick up our
pieces, rebuild and come back stronger than ever.

_____

_____

_____

_____

_____

December 5

□ □ □ □ □

Make your dreams a size too big and grow into them. Today is your day. Go slow or fast – either way you'll get there. Trust in what you know and who you are.

_____

_____

_____

_____

_____

December 6

□ □ □ □ □

You can't keep expecting others to be more than you're willing to be. It is ok for anyone not to be perfect – set the pace and work together.

_____

_____

_____

_____

_____

December 7

□ □ □ □ □

There comes a time when you must realize you don't have to impress anyone. They will love you for who you are or they won't. That is not your worry. Be amazing. The right ones will automatically gravitate to you.

_____

_____

_____

_____

_____

December 8

□ □ □ □ □

You aren't a trophy or a prize; you are strong but delicate. You are meant to be treasured. Don't settle for less.

_____

_____

_____

_____

_____

December 9

□ □ □ □ □

An experience to reach in and tickle all of our senses – that is what we all want, but so few are willing to take the leap for it.

_____

_____

_____

_____

_____

December 10

□ □ □ □ □

Naturally, we display our feelings with those we are most comfortable with. Surround yourself with the ones that feel the same. Be ridiculously amazing.

_____

_____

_____

_____

_____

December 11

☐ ☐ ☐ ☐ ☐

Those that encourage you to be your best but love
and accept you at your worst, those are your
people. Keep them close.

_____

_____

_____

_____

_____

December 12

☐ ☐ ☐ ☐ ☐

Be so busy loving life there is no time for hate,
regret or despair.
If you can't do great big things, then do great
little things.
Think like there is no box at all.

_____

_____

_____

_____

_____

December 13

□ □ □ □ □

Love can melt the hardest of hearts, heal the broken and quiet fear. Trust in it.

_____

_____

_____

_____

_____

December 14

□ □ □ □ □

I am a wild lover, passion engulfs me.
The fire in my soul burns deep.
My kisses will ignite your love.
My eyes stare into your depths.
I will break you; I will fix you.
Through no choice of your own – I am yours.
I am addictive.

_____

_____

_____

_____

_____

December 15

□ □ □ □ □

Sometimes a problem doesn't require solving, but
instead maturity to outgrow it.
Failure doesn't define you, determination does.

_____

_____

_____

_____

_____

December 16

□ □ □ □ □

Your past is just that; you don't live there
anymore. Learn from it.
Your future isn't here yet; dream, hope and plan
for it.
Your present is now; get busy living it.
Don't make a permanent decision based on
temporary feelings. It makes regret.
Love without limits – trust your heart.

_____

_____

_____

_____

_____

December 17

□ □ □ □ □

Your talent is God given. Be humble and use it.
Our fame is man given. Be grateful and show it.
One's conceit is self-given. Be careful.

_____

_____

_____

_____

_____

December 18

□ □ □ □ □

Freedom is letting go of what others want from
you and being what you were meant to be without
fear.

_____

_____

_____

_____

_____

December 19

□ □ □ □ □

Life is change – Growth is optional.
Take hold and move mountains.

_____

_____

_____

_____

_____

_____

December 20

□ □ □ □ □

The problem is not the problem. The problem is
your attitude about the problem.
Live more, Complain less,
More smiles, Less stress,
Less hate, More love.

_____

_____

_____

_____

_____

December 21

□ □ □ □ □

Be miserable or motivate yourself, it is always yours to make. If you want to fly, you have to give up what weighs you down.

_____

_____

_____

_____

_____

December 22

□ □ □ □ □

Life is about laughing and living, replacing inner hate with love, getting through whatever comes your way and looking back and smiling at it all.

_____

_____

_____

_____

_____

December 23

☐ ☐ ☐ ☐ ☐

Be Happy, Love with all you have and Smile Often.

_____

_____

_____

_____

_____

_____

December 24

☐ ☐ ☐ ☐ ☐

Love is not how you forget, but, rather, how you
forgive.
Not what you hear, but perceive as meaning.
Not how you walk away, but how you stay with
everything you are fighting for.
It is never how big the house is, but how happy you
are in it.

_____

_____

_____

_____

_____

December 25

□ □ □ □ □

A good laugh and a long sleep, never underestimate
the power of both.

_____

_____

_____

_____

_____

_____

December 26

□ □ □ □ □

I have learned to be thankful in my struggles
because they taught me my strength. Someday,
we'll know exactly why it had to happen.

_____

_____

_____

_____

_____

December 27

□ □ □ □ □

Decide today you will live by choice, not chance.
Go forth making changes, not excuses.
Choose to listen to your voice, not the voice of the
world.

_____

_____

_____

_____

_____

December 28

□ □ □ □ □

Life is tough but so are YOU.
Smile and accomplish!

_____

_____

_____

_____

_____

December 29

□ □ □ □ □

I think I fall in love in the tiniest of ways with
anyone willing to show me their soul. This world is
so guarded and aloof, I welcome the raw openness
and all it stands for.

_____

_____

_____

_____

_____

December 30

□ □ □ □ □

It is not enough to be compassionate, you must act.
Forgiveness does not change our past it just gives
us peace and enlarges our future. To wish you were
someone else is to waste who you are.......climb the
mountain so you can see the world not so the world
can see you.

_____

_____

_____

_____

_____

December 31

□ □ □ □ □

You should always listen with your head to have knowledge, your heart to understand, and both to do the right thing.

_____

_____

_____

_____

_____